D0501553

ENTREPRENEURIAL STRENGTHSFINDER

JIM CLIFTON

Chairman of Gallup and Author of *The Coming Jobs War*

SANGEETA BHARADWAJ BADAL, Ph.D.

GALLUP PRESS
1251 Avenue of the Americas
23rd Floor
New York, NY 10020

Library of Congress Control Number: 2013949878
ISBN: 978-1-59562-082-8   *5498 3571*   */14*

First Printing: 2014
10 9 8 7 6 5 4 3 2 1

Printed in Canada

*To the city leaders who are transforming
America and the world — one city at a time*

TABLE OF CONTENTS

PART 1

ONLY ENTREPRENEURS CAN SAVE AMERICA AND THE WORLD

by Jim Clifton

DEAD WRONG ECONOMIC ASSUMPTIONS

During my 40 years at Gallup, I've observed that when very talented leaders fail, it's often because their thinking failed them. Not their management or leadership skills, but their thinking about a core belief that they put at the center of all of their strategies. Because they are so wrong about that core belief, every subsequent decision actually makes things worse, because every decision is tied to that belief. The more they manage and lead, the worse things get.

This is happening in Washington, D.C., but it is also happening in many cities throughout America.

Let me illustrate. Thirty years ago, a colleague and I conducted a project in a Midwestern city for a group of talented investors and businesspeople. This was a time when McDonald's franchises were growing quickly, and these businesspeople wanted to copy the fast-food chain's success. They came to the conclusion that McDonald's business was soaring because of one key attribute: speed of service. That was their belief.

So these smart, talented people built everything around this core belief about speed, and they committed to delivering food faster. Pneumatic tubes shot the food to the customer, and the company touted its service as the fastest. They even named the chain "Chutes."

Now, they did get hamburgers and fries to their customers faster than McDonald's did. They achieved their goal. But they discovered too late that the primary reason McDonald's was exploding was because customers loved the taste of the food — especially the french fries. Speed was not the core reason McDonald's customers ate there; the taste of the food was. Chutes' core assumption was wrong. The more they executed on their belief, the worse things got.

I've seen hundreds of mistakes like that one, but here's one with far bigger implications. Many people in the highest levels of U.S. government think that the 1.5 billion Muslims in the world hate the West for our freedom and that religion divides us. Leaders build policy — war, economic sanctions, and anti-terror campaigns — around these assumptions. But Gallup World Poll data tell another story entirely.

The world's Muslims don't hate us because of our freedom or because they're religious fanatics. Gallup finds that their discomfort originates predominantly from a hopelessness rooted in economic despair — and especially joblessness — that for some, manifests in violence. This is an economic problem, a respect problem, a dignity problem. Not a religious problem.

Before Tunisian food vendor Mohammed Bouazizi set himself on fire, thus igniting the current and continuously exploding Arab Spring, he didn't yell, "Death to America!" or "Allahu akbar!" He cried out, "I just want to work!" The police had taken his food cart away from him — his means of earning a living — and he set himself on fire because of his relationship to a job, not his relationship to Allah or America.

What Bouazizi did struck a nerve throughout the Middle East and set off a regional revolution. Nonetheless, too often, Western policies aren't built to fix unemployment and subsequent hopelessness. And the more mistaken the foreign policy assumptions that we act on are, the worse we make the world.

I am starting with these two stories because leaders — business leaders, nonprofit leaders, political leaders, teachers, NGO leaders, coaches, and mentors to millions of American youths and adults — need to be open to the possibility that many of the core premises of U.S. leadership are dead wrong. And the policy that U.S. leadership is most wrong about is how jobs are created. We're so seriously misguided in our thinking about how jobs are born that we're running the risk of putting our country on a course of permanent decline.

The "how to fix America" theory that virtually all leaders subscribe to today — their core, strategy-defining belief — is that jobs and economic growth are conceived by *innovation*. The premise is that *great ideas and inventions* drive economies, that new businesses spring from those ideas, and then somehow, new, good jobs magically appear right afterward.

American leaders have bet everything — the entire republic — on the premise of innovation.

But what if they're dead wrong? What if this is their Chutes mistake? What if they are missing the point, as leaders did when the Arab Spring erupted? What if the whole world is wrong about how jobs are created?

Here's what leaders need to know: Jobs and GDP growth *do not* predictably follow innovation. Jobs and GDP growth *do* predictably follow entrepreneurship. Put another way: Entrepreneurs create customers. And customers, in turn, create jobs and economic growth. Almost no leader knows this.

Global conventional wisdom says that America became a world colossus because of spectacular innovation. Thousands of conferences and organizations around the world were built on this assumption. Some countries are even building "innovation cities." But the problem is, the "innovation assumption" doesn't hold up.

Virtually all U.S. and world leaders have misdiagnosed the core problem and put billions and billions of dollars into mistaken strategies that are not helping America's economy, much less the world's.

Innovation is essential, and we need it. But the real magic starts with entrepreneurs — with people who are born with the rare gift to build successful businesses.

ENTREPRENEURSHIP VS. INNOVATION

It's absolutely critical that leaders understand this: An innovation has no value until an ambitious entrepreneur builds a business model around it and turns it into a product or service that customers will buy. If you can't turn an innovative idea into something that creates a customer, it's worthless.

But first, a quick but important distinction between innovators and entrepreneurs. An innovator is first and foremost a creator, a problem solver with a deep passion for improving something. Innovators are *thinkers*. But an entrepreneur is driven to act, to build. This includes building the businesses that make and sell the things that innovators think up, because entrepreneurs are *doers*.

Of course we need innovators. And we need tons of their ideas and innovations. But we need to ask the right question about every single one of those ideas: "Can we sell it?" Every time an inventor has a new idea, we should ask, "Exactly who is the customer?" "What miracle does it provide the customer?" "What is the business model?" "How many customers will love this?"

Putting tens of billions more dollars into innovation is like stacking a wood pile higher and higher with no matches to strike the fire. That is the current strategy of virtually all American leaders, national and local — just piling the stack of valueless innovation higher and higher. We mean well, but it isn't getting us where we think it will.

Thought leaders often ask me: Aren't innovation and entrepreneurship like the chicken and the egg? Which really comes first? My answer is: That's the wrong analogy. The right one is the cart and the horse. Entrepreneurship is the horse, and innovation is the cart. In putting innovation ahead of entrepreneurship, our thinking has been dangerously off. It doesn't matter how brilliant the innovative idea is if there's no one to create a business that sells it.

Because America's core economic premise is based on new ideas rather than on new businesses, the country just keeps loading the cart with more and more innovation. What the U.S. needs instead is a team of horses to pull the best ideas into the marketplace.

Almost no one in Washington understands this. Innovation, discovery, breakthroughs, ideas, and creativity are valuable and necessary — we can't get enough of them. But they create little to no economic energy in and of themselves until an almighty customer appears. The car, the light bulb, flight, the transistor, and the Internet created little to no economic energy until each invention was successfully commercialized — until customers appeared.

So our real problem is not that there isn't enough innovation. It's that there aren't enough entrepreneurs starting new businesses. The U.S. now ranks not first, not second, not third, but 12th among developed nations in terms of startup activity. Countries such as Hungary, Denmark, Finland, New Zealand, Sweden, Israel, and Italy all have higher startup rates than America does. We are behind in starting new firms per capita, and this is our single most serious economic problem. Yet it seems like a secret. You never see it mentioned in the media, nor hear from a politician that, for the first time in 35 years, American business deaths now outnumber business births.

The U.S. Census Bureau reports that the total number of new business startups and business closures per year — the birth and death rates of American companies — have just crossed for the first time since the measurement began. I am referring to employer businesses, those with one or more employees, the real engines of economic growth. Four hundred thousand new businesses are being born annually nationwide, while 470,000 per year are dying.

The deaths of businesses now outnumber the births of businesses.

This will be the first time you have seen this graph.

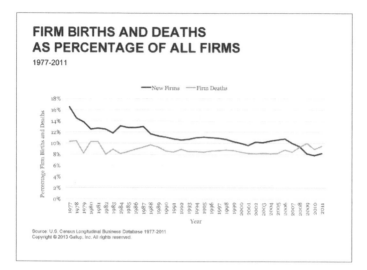

FIRM BIRTHS AND DEATHS
AS PERCENTAGE OF ALL FIRMS
1977-2011

Until 2008, startups outpaced business failures by about 100,000 per year. But in the past six years, that number suddenly turned upside down. There has been an underground earthquake. As you read this, we are at minus 70,000 in terms of business survival. The data are very slow coming out of the U.S. Department of Census, via the Small Business Administration, so it lags real time by two years.

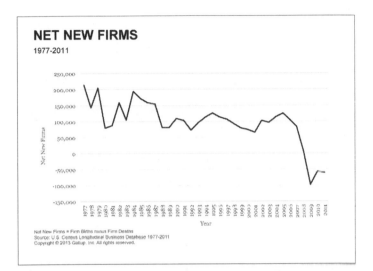

NET NEW FIRMS
1977-2011

Net New Firms = Firm Births minus Firm Deaths
Source: U.S. Census Longitudinal Business Database 1977-2011
Copyright © 2013 Gallup, Inc. All rights reserved.

My hunch is that no one talks about the birth and death rates of American business because Wall Street and the White House, no matter which party occupies the latter, are two gigantic institutions of persuasion. The White House needs to keep you in the game because their political party needs your vote. Wall Street needs the stock market to boom, even if that boom is fueled by illusion. So both tell us, "The economy is coming back."

Let's get one thing clear: This economy is never coming back unless we reverse the birth and death trends of American businesses.

It is catastrophic to be dead wrong on the biggest issue of the last 50 years — the issue of where jobs come from. Current thinking tells us we're on the right track and don't need different strategies, so we continue marching down the path of national decline.

I don't want to sound like a doomsayer, but when small and medium-sized businesses are dying faster than they're being born, so is free enterprise. And when free enterprise dies, America dies with it.

Let's run some numbers. You will often hear from otherwise credible sources that there are 26 million businesses in America. This is misleading; 20 million of these reported "businesses" are inactive companies that have no sales, profits, customers, or workers. The only number that is useful and instructive is the number of current operating businesses with one or more employees.

There are only 6 million businesses in the United States with one or more employees. Of those, 3.8 million have four or fewer employees — mom and pop shops owned by people who aren't building a business as much as they are building a life. And God bless them all. That is what America is for. We need every single one of them.

Next, there are about a million companies with five to nine employees, 600,000 businesses with 10 to 19 employees, and 500,000 companies with 20 to 99 employees. There are 90,000 businesses with 100 to 499 employees. And there are just 18,000 with 500 employees or more, and that figure includes about a thousand companies with 10,000 employees or more. Altogether, that is America, Inc.

Let me be very clear. America, Inc. is far more important to America's security than our military. Because without the former prospering — and solvent — there is no latter. We have enormous military power only because of a growing economy that has, so far, made it possible for the government to pay its bills. When former Chairman of the Joint Chiefs of Staff, Adm. Mike Mullen, was asked in a Senate hearing on June 28, 2011, to name the biggest current threat to the security of the United States, he didn't say al-Qaida. He didn't say Iran's nuclear capabilities. He answered, "I believe our debt is the greatest threat to our national security."

Keep in mind that these 6 million businesses, especially small and medium-sized ones, provide jobs for more than 100 million Americans and much of the tax base for everything. These small, medium, and big businesses have generated the biggest economy in the world, which has allowed the country to afford lavish military and social spending and entitlements. And we've been able to afford all of this because, until now, we've dominated the world economy.

When new businesses aren't being born, the free enterprise system and jobs decline. And without a growing free enterprise system, without a growing entrepreneurial economy, there are no new good jobs. That means declining revenues and smaller salaries to tax, followed by declining aid for the elderly and poor and declining funding for the military, for education, for infrastructure — declining revenues for everything.

America has maintained the biggest tax coffers in the world because its 300+ million citizens have produced and owned one-quarter of virtually all global wealth. The United States clobbered everyone in the battle of free enterprise, in the battle of business building, and in the battle of inventing the future. Until recently, America had blown the world away in terms of economic success. We are now quickly losing that edge, and everything we're trying to do to fix the problem is dead wrong.

Here's why: Entrepreneurship is not systematically built into our culture the way innovation or intellectual development is. You might say, "Well, I see a lot of entrepreneurial activity in the country." Yes, that's true, but entrepreneurship is now in decline for the first time since the U.S. government started measuring it.

The whole country and subsequently the world are having their own dead-wrong moment, and it is causing America and the whole world to make everything worse. And people know it, though they may not know why. As Gallup recently reported, when asked to name their "greatest worry or concern about the future of the United States," 34% of respondents said the economy, the nation's finances, or unemployment/jobs. Losing freedom and civil liberties was a top concern of only 4% of Americans, and immigration and border control garnered 2%. Gay marriage and the environment didn't even make the list.

The more we execute on our leadership's erroneous belief in innovation, the more our engine stalls out.

The American economy recently experienced the worst ever GDP growth in its history, which has hurt global human development. Global economic growth, as I write today, is slipping too — from 5.3% in 2010 to less than 3% in 2013 — which means we don't have enough incoming economic juice to provide badly needed new jobs around the world, let alone prevent more instability and revolutions.

Because we have misdiagnosed the cause and effect of economic growth, we have misdiagnosed the cause and effect of job creation. To get back on track, we need to quit pinning everything on innovation, and we need to start focusing on the almighty entrepreneurs and business builders. And that means we have to find them.

LEFT TO CHANCE: FINDING RARE ENTREPRENEURIAL TALENT

If you have a high IQ, America's massive testing systems will find you. We're probably the best in the world at high-level intellectual development. There is no chance a really smart student will be overlooked in America.

If you have the rare, innate talent to play basketball or football, our massive youth-to-college-to-pro sports systems will find you. We're probably the best in the world at early identification and development of star athletes. There is no chance a sports star will be missed in America.

However, if you have the rare, innate ability to create a customer, to build a company — if you have the talent for entrepreneurship — your early identification and subsequent development is left to chance. If you possess star "business builder" brilliance, you will likely be overlooked in America.

The U.S. has no peer at developing students with high IQs. Our country is home to most of the best universities in the world. And the best of America's top private and public K-12 schools do a world-class job at accelerating smart kids.

Right now, a student in fifth through 12th grade who is blessed with an unusually high IQ will be spotted. Whether you live in Philadelphia or Tacoma, on a poor farm in a desolate area of Texas or in Nebraska, if you have a genius-level aptitude for learning, our testing system will sort you out, and your life will start changing and developing quickly.

My dad, Don Clifton, was born on a sheep ranch in northern Nebraska. It was there that county-level tests discovered that he was an unusual learner and thinker. He was offered a scholarship to the University of Nebraska, and he stayed there, teaching educational psychology and researching what he called "strengths theory." That theory became the Clifton StrengthsFinder assessment, and it changed the world.

So the system worked for Dad. It found him in the middle of nowhere raising sheep and reading and learning like crazy, and that was 75 years ago. The system still works. If you were blessed with an unusual gift to learn, we will find you. And we will teach you and support you and wait anxiously for your book smarts to grow and develop.

But if you were born with the very rare talent, born with a unique neuron configuration for entrepreneurship, born with the genius to create customers, you're pretty much on your own.

We certainly won't find you in Compton or Queens or Amarillo. You might have access to a random special class for entrepreneurs, but there is no formal early identification system, no colleges bidding for you, no national benchmarks for ranking rare individuals like you. Colleges and universities place tremendous weight on SAT or ACT scores, but nobody asks about the applicant's entrepreneurial aptitude to start a company, build an organization, or create millions of customers. We don't know how someone like that works at all.

However, Gallup research strongly suggests that entrepreneurs have innate traits that make them successful. Let me make this really clear: Nature trumps nurture as far as entrepreneurship goes. Entrepreneurs are born, they learn to use their innate talents, and then they succeed. The ones who become superstars — Richard Branson, Mark Zuckerberg, and Sara Blakely, to name a few — are the ones who had innate talent and were able to make the most of that talent.

But millions more entrepreneurs don't know what to do with the talent God gave them. They may not even know they have entrepreneurial talent at all, because there is no formal system for identifying them.

All talents, of any kind, explode with early identification and intentional development. But the talent for entrepreneurship doesn't receive the close attention that we routinely offer, even to middle school cheerleaders.

The single most important factor for America's economic survival remains as mysterious as life on Mars. But maybe that's because it's so unusual. Preliminary Gallup research discovered that high entrepreneurial talent is much rarer than high IQ: Only about five in 1,000 people have the aptitude for starting and growing a big business. In comparison, 20 in 1,000 have IQs high enough to be accepted into Mensa.

Imagine how the world would change if we recorded and reported aptitude scores for entrepreneurial talent — if the U.S. could identify those with the right talent and get them into accelerated development programs in the best schools. The day when there is a list of "blue-chip" potential entrepreneurs coming out of your local high schools and colleges is the day when America, and subsequently the world, will change forever. Conversations will change. Leadership will change.

City and national strategies will change. Billions of dollars' worth of investments will change. A very specific human talent will have new value and respect, because we can intentionally direct and control economic energy and subsequently the future of cities and nations.

FORGET WASHINGTON: CITIES WILL WIN OR LOSE AMERICA

Finding blue-chip entrepreneurs is not the federal government's responsibility. It has to happen at the city level because most economic activity of any significance occurs there. The reality is, when it comes to creating economic growth and good jobs, local leadership is far more important than national leadership. This is largely because cities, like companies, exhibit wide variation in economic outcomes.

There are examples of this variation all around the country. Austin and Albany are both capital cities in big American states. Neither city is located by a port or a natural tourist attraction with beaches or mountains. They're pretty much alike, except that economically speaking, Austin wins big and Albany loses big. One city is a drain on America, and the other continues to save it. Sioux Falls is booming, while Sioux City is not. Think how different Detroit's outcomes are from San Francisco's. Detroit went from being one of the richest cities in the world to being one of the most spectacular failures. One could even make the argument that citizens in the San Francisco area saved the republic and national job creation by leading the tech-entrepreneurship boom.

The difference, in my view, is that Austin, Sioux Falls, and San Francisco have deeply caring and highly engaged business, political, and philanthropic leaders. Those leaders understand how to build a thriving, growing economy — one that welcomes business and entrepreneurship. Albany, Sioux City, and Detroit have the opposite: leaders with principles, policies, values, and beliefs that discourage business and entrepreneurship, if not outright scare them away.

The good news is, strong leadership teams are already in place within cities — even failing ones. A natural order is already present, in governments and local business and philanthropic entities. Every city has strong, caring leaders working on numerous committees and initiatives to fuel their local economic growth and to create good jobs. Those leaders should attract innovators, yes, but they'll fail if they don't identify and develop entrepreneurs as well. Simply put, local leaders have to find out who in their town is a high-potential, blue-chip entrepreneur with the God-given talent to build a big, booming business.

A big part of this effort is getting local businesses involved as well as aligning the strategies and will of all the great local organizations, such as Junior Achievement, 4-H Club, DECA, Lemonade Day, Operation HOPE, and so on. To find and develop blue-chip entrepreneurs, America needs all institutions and organizations involved.

Ultimately, the war for jobs and sudden economic growth will be fought city by city around the world — San Francisco vs. Seoul, Brooklyn vs. Berlin. Each city needs its own highly individualized plan because each city has its own unique entrepreneurial talent — and each must find it, maximize it, and retain it. Early identification of rare entrepreneurial talent will be the most significant turning point in recent human history. And this talent is out there today, undiscovered.

There are nearly 30 million students in U.S. middle and high schools right now. Early Gallup research reports that about five in 1,000 working-age adults in the U.S. possess the rare talents of entrepreneurship, so that means there are about 150,000 future blue-chip entrepreneurs in fifth through 12th grade now, more in college, and tens of thousands more adult potential business builders out there. City leaders should find them all and make their entrepreneurial growth as systematic and intentional as intellectual and athletic growth are. Great business builders are like great scientists or great quarterbacks — they will respond and accelerate with high-quality attention. Furthermore, without it, their potential is at risk of being underdeveloped, or worse, never developed at all.

The potential of these individuals is unlimited in terms of the economic fortunes they can and will bring to your city. As off-track as our American future appears today, a sudden spectacular turnaround is 100% doable if we change our leadership's thinking and strategies.

Keep in mind that the percentage who can develop new booming businesses is much larger than 0.5%. We estimate that an additional 2% of the adult population possesses the inherent traits and talents to build a business of some size and substance. And we need them all.

Whether the U.S. goes broke or suddenly booms lies predominantly in the American phenomenon of small and medium-sized business startups and their subsequent explosion. America will re-win the world only when entrepreneurs build new empires of customers and jobs and create unlimited economic growth for their cities and countries.

WE CAN NOW IDENTIFY FUTURE ENTREPRENEURS

Later in the book, my colleague Sangeeta Bharadwaj Badal will explain in detail the traits, drives, and innate talents that rare business builders possess — what Gallup calls the 10 talents of successful entrepreneurs. She will also introduce you to Gallup's Entrepreneurial StrengthsFinder, the first-ever comprehensive assessment that identifies who has what it takes to start and build big businesses.

Gallup worked with the best test makers in the world, primarily our own, but also with well-known academics in the field, including the late Harvard professor Phil Stone, to create the first in-depth assessment for entrepreneurial talent. We are confident that the God-given attributes of entrepreneurship are as testable as the vertical jump. Our first entrepreneurial assessment is done, and it will help change the future of your city, country, and all humankind.

PART 2

WHAT CITY LEADERS SHOULD DO NOW

by Jim Clifton

City leaders have to be deadly serious about new business startups and entrepreneurship. The future of your city — and the fate of the American economy, not to mention the country's standing in the world — depend on it. Half of all jobs are in small businesses, according to the Small Business Administration, and they create approximately 65% of all new jobs.

Here's what leaders have to do to create a culture of entrepreneurship in their cities:

- **Install an early identification assessment system.** Using the Entrepreneurial StrengthsFinder (ESF) assessment, test thousands of students — from freshmen in high school to sophomores in college. Everyone who takes the assessment should attend a group learning session about entrepreneurship and discuss their results.

- **Establish an accelerated development program.** The students with the highest potential should participate in a special prestigious program. Create a committee for selecting students into it. The program should include:

- **Specialized curriculum:** Students should spend some to all of their time in special classes focused on entrepreneurship.

- **Meaningful internships:** Students should work as interns in community businesses to get hands-on experience in a real enterprise — and they should be paid.

- **Certified coaches:** Students should participate in regular one-on-one coaching sessions with Gallup-certified ESF coaches. Coaching sessions should be focused on development of individual talents.

Your city's destiny — and America's — will no longer be determined just by fiscal policy, job legislation, and tax rates, but by whether it inspires a spirit of free enterprise and connects that spirit directly to desperately needed local GDP growth. How effectively you can draw the local spirit of free enterprise — a culture of entrepreneurship — out of your young people will determine the number of startups in your city, the creation of good jobs, and eventually whether your city has the money and resources for anything else that matters.

PART 3

THE 10 TALENTS OF SUCCESSFUL ENTREPRENEURS

by Sangeeta Bharadwaj Badal, Ph.D.

Finding the World's Most Talented Business Builders

What separates successful business owners from less successful ones?

What are the traits and behaviors that drive an individual to start, sustain, and grow a successful company?

How does the psychology of entrepreneurs influence their decision making?

Do entrepreneurial attitudes toward autonomy, risk, work, and income affect business outcomes?

Are the personality characteristics required to create a venture different from those that facilitate a venture's expansion and growth?

Intrigued by these questions and many others, Gallup studied 2,500 entrepreneurs to understand the actions and decisions that lead to venture creation and growth. After years of research and hundreds of interviews, Gallup has identified 10 specific talents that drive business success —

10 behaviors we consistently observed in highly successful entrepreneurs.

In this section, I will elaborate on the 10 essential talents of business builders with the hope that if you are planning to start a business or are managing one, you can discover your entrepreneurial talents and, in the process, increase your odds of success.

Before I dive into the 10 talents, let me start by explaining why and how the psychology of the entrepreneur affects business outcomes.

Linking Talent to Business Outcomes

Ronald Perelman, the CEO and chairman of MacAndrews & Forbes Holdings, recently committed $100 million to the Columbia Business School to teach the next generation how to become entrepreneurs — more on whether we can teach someone to be an entrepreneur later. Even though the school will use the funds to create courses on entrepreneurship that teach a person the skills to successfully manage a business, Perelman acknowledges that entrepreneurship is based on one's "gut instinct." He goes on to describe gut instinct as one of those things you either have or you don't.

Gut instinct is a term used to explain what you feel intuitively or instinctively about something — a recurring pattern of thought, feeling, or behavior dependent on the circuitry of your brain. The intricate wiring of the brain differs from person to person and determines our unique personality and preferences.

Our basic personality characteristics are a function of our brain circuitry, enduring and stable over time and across different situations. This consistency of personality traits allows us to predict broad classes of individual behaviors. You can learn who a person is by observing his or her behaviors because there is an underlying consistent thread in those behaviors based on his or her personality traits.

As far back as the 1930s, economists like Irving Fisher and John Maynard Keynes have studied the link between personality characteristics and economic behavior. Since then, research has clearly established positive significant relationships between different personality characteristics or talents — need for achievement, risk propensity, passion, creativity, autonomy, and self-efficacy — and entrepreneurial outcomes such as sales and profit.

Let me share some examples. Researchers at the department of psychology at the University of Giessen, Germany, found that self-efficacy — belief in one's ability to do a task well — has a high correlation to business creation and success. In fact, they found that the correlation between self-efficacy and business success was as high as the correlation between the weight and height of adults in the U.S. — one of the highest medical correlations. High self-efficacy motivates an individual to take initiative, persevere in the face of resistance, and have self-confidence and a hopeful outlook for the future — behaviors that lead to venture success.

Similarly, other researchers have found a strong correlation between achievement orientation (a personal desire for achievement) and business success. Entrepreneurs with a strong desire for achievement set high standards for themselves and others around them. They constantly look for better ways to accomplish a task. They anticipate problems and are willing to take risks to achieve their goals. These talents trigger behaviors that ultimately lead to business success.

Researchers have also extensively studied the relationship between risk taking and business success. Risk-takers are likely to try something adventurous or to take a gamble. They thrive in high-stakes environments and have a higher propensity to engage in risky ventures. In entrepreneurship, this translates into an overly optimistic perception of risk. This helps them start a business or take an existing business to the next level. Risk-tolerant individuals are likely to thrive in complexity, uncertainty, and urgency. No obstacle is too great and no challenge is too difficult for them. They are likely to invest in new projects and explore new markets when people who are more risk-averse may be paralyzed by fear of the unknown.

Over the last few years, Gallup's assessment of 2,500 U.S. entrepreneurs found that higher levels of entrepreneurial talent significantly increase one's odds of business success. Highly talented entrepreneurs, compared with their less talented peers, are:

- three times more likely to build large businesses and to grow them significantly
- four times more likely to create jobs
- four times more likely to exceed profit goals
- five times more likely to exceed sales goals

In another study of 111 small businesses in Nebraska, Gallup found that highly talented entrepreneurs exhibited distinctive behaviors. These behaviors caused the highly talented entrepreneurs to outperform others by 22 percentage points in year-over-year profit growth. Compared with their less talented peers, highly talented entrepreneurs:

- were more likely to clearly articulate the competitive advantage of their companies to their clients

- were more likely to make decisions about pricing and product or service development with their customers in mind

- spent a great deal more time planning for growth and aligning employee responsibilities with company goals

- were more likely to align employees' strengths with their roles, thus maximizing employee engagement and increasing individual performance

As you can see from these studies, there is a clear positive relationship between entrepreneurial talents and business creation and success. Business-building talent affects behaviors that in turn influence entrepreneurial outcomes.

Entrepreneurial Talent: Innate or Learned?

An example of two violinists with differing levels of talent can help answer the question about whether entrepreneurial talent is innate or learned. Sally has an innate ability to identify the pitch and tone of a musical composition. By the age of five, she could learn music by ear and created perfect first drafts of her compositions. She has precise rhythmic ability and can reproduce an exact musical note without an external reference. Martha, Sally's classmate since elementary school, has a keen sense of music but lacks some of Sally's innate musical abilities.

Irma Järvelä, a medical geneticist at the University of Helsinki, and her colleagues found that about 50% of musical ability is heritable (genetic). In other words, nature accounts for almost half of the observed differences in musical ability. This means Sally has an innate advantage over Martha.

High levels of innate talent do not mean that deliberate practice and hard work are unimportant.

Rigorous practice, self-motivation, and support from family members, mentors, and teachers will certainly help both violinists fully realize their musical ability. But Sally, with greater natural talent for music, will see much greater returns compared with Martha, who has less natural musical ability.

Similarly, in the realm of entrepreneurship, innate talents seem to make some people better at noticing new business opportunities and more likely to be risk-takers, natural salespeople, and adept at cultivating social networks — all traits that drive entrepreneurial success. If you do not have these traits, you could try to learn the behaviors associated with a trait or take business classes, but Gallup's research suggests that you would have to do a considerable amount of work and might still achieve only average performance.

Business support programs can teach you basic management, accounting and finance, or marketing skills. They can provide technical assistance. Mentors and coaches can give you advice, share their own experiences, and be your support system through the entrepreneurial journey. But support programs and coaches cannot teach you to recognize opportunities or to become a risk-taker. Nor can they teach you how to best use social networks to further your business interests. Just as genetics has a role in someone's musical ability, Nicos Nicolaou of Cass Business School, City University London, and Scott Shane of Case Western Reserve University found that the tendency toward entrepreneurship is between 37% and 48% genetic.

In sum, you are likely to be most successful when working with your dominant natural talents. Training and education will certainly help you achieve excellence in an entrepreneurial role, but success will come easier if you have an inherent talent for the role. This means that identifying your entrepreneurial potential is critical. After identifying your potential, you need to apply systematic and continuous effort to nurture your innate ability and to manage your areas of lesser ability.

Identifying Entrepreneurial Talent

If innate talents are strong predictors of behaviors that affect business outcomes, then it follows that we can study individuals' behavior, identify their intensity of entrepreneurial talent, and then support them to speed the process of venture creation and growth.

During our research, we found a tremendous variety of behaviors among successful entrepreneurs. For instance, successful entrepreneurs effortlessly cultivate deep relationships with customers and employees (trait = interpersonal), are laser-focused on business outcomes (trait = thought process), are creative problem solvers (trait = creative thinking), and are the best spokespeople for their businesses (trait = promotion).

But after analyzing the data and listening to hours of interviews, we distilled everything down to a list of 10 talents that influence behaviors and best explain success in an entrepreneurial role. Every entrepreneur uses some mix of these 10 talents to start or grow a business.

The 10 talents of successful entrepreneurs are:

Business Focus: You make decisions based on observed or anticipated effect on profit.

Confidence: You accurately know yourself and understand others.

Creative Thinker: You exhibit creativity in taking an existing idea or product and turning it into something better.

Delegator: You recognize that you cannot do everything and are willing to contemplate a shift in style and control.

Determination: You persevere through difficult, even seemingly insurmountable, obstacles.

Independent: You are prepared to do whatever needs to be done to build a successful venture.

Knowledge-Seeker: You constantly search for information that is relevant to growing your business.

Promoter: You are the best spokesperson for the business.

Relationship-Builder: You have high social awareness and an ability to build relationships that are beneficial for the firm's survival and growth.

Risk-Taker: You instinctively know how to manage high-risk situations.

The degree of your natural ability in each of the 10 talents will determine where you will be successful and where you will fall short in your entrepreneurial journey. There are three levels of ability for each talent: dominant, contributing, and supporting. You consistently and naturally lead with your **dominant talents.** You show some evidence of your **contributing talents,** but you must deliberately apply them to achieve success. Finally, the talents that you don't naturally lead with are your **supporting talents.**

Pay special attention to your dominant talents, and use them to your advantage. Be aware of your contributing talents, but do not spend too much time on them. Look for partners or put strategies in place to manage these talents. Finally, reinforce your supporting talents with partnerships and support from others. For example, if building relationships is your forte, but focusing on business or sales is not, put your energy into forming and cultivating networks that can propel your business to the next level, and leave sales and numbers to someone who is good at them.

These 10 talents, or drivers of entrepreneurial success, are additive. In other words, if you have dominant talent in six areas, your likelihood of entrepreneurial success is significantly higher compared with someone who has dominant levels of talent in only four. If you are strong in seven areas, your chances of success increase even further, and so on. This is important because the more areas you are strong in, the more business outcomes you can influence —

and each talent affects specific business outcomes. For instance, those with dominant talent in Business Focus are twice as likely to exceed their profit goals. Those with dominant talent in Determination are twice as likely to exceed sales goals. And those with dominant Risk-Taker talent are four times more likely to grow their business significantly.

Dominant talent in all 10 areas is rare but predicts the highest chance of success for an entrepreneur. While only 5 in 1,000 working-age adults in the U.S. have high talent across all 10 areas, many entrepreneurs with fewer dominant talents are still very successful. To increase your likelihood of success, identify strategies to manage areas of weakness, or acquire skills and knowledge to deal with your contributing or supporting talents. Or best of all, form partnerships with people who have a different set of talents.

These 10 talents do not address every factor that affects business success. Non-personality variables such as skills, knowledge, and experience along with a host of external factors play a role in determining business success and must be taken into consideration when theorizing on business creation and success. But these 10 talents explain a large part of entrepreneurial success and cannot and should not be ignored. Understanding and acknowledging your inherent talents gives you the best chance at success.

To help you find your unique mix of these 10 talents, Gallup created an online assessment called Entrepreneurial StrengthsFinder. If you haven't already done so, go to www.gallupstrengthscenter. com to take the assessment before reading the chapters ahead. You will need the unique access code in the packet in the back of this book to take the assessment. After you complete the assessment, you will receive a report with your unique talent profile. Your customized results enable you to discover your entrepreneurial talents, understand how each will play out in your entrepreneurial journey, and learn how to make the most of this information to start or grow your business.

In addition to your unique profile, you will receive the Gallup Entrepreneurial StrengthsFinder Report Guide that includes:

1. interpretation of your results

2. strategies for developing your entrepreneurial talents

3. an action plan that helps you apply your talents to building your business

Do not use the results of this assessment to determine whether you should or should not become an entrepreneur. Instead, let the results guide you along the entrepreneurial journey, and learn how to use your talents to be the best entrepreneur and business builder you can be. Use your profile to create a strategy map to build on your talents and to identify performance gaps, if any, between your potential, competencies, and the needs of the role.

Focus your energy on developing your natural talents. They are the key to the survival and success of your venture. On the other hand, be aware of your weaknesses or challenges. Manage them by implementing systems, acquiring skills and knowledge, or establishing complementary partnerships.

Who Should Use the Assessment, Book, and Guide?

As my colleague Jim Clifton says earlier in the book, large-scale change happens at the city level. City leaders must encourage budding entrepreneurs waiting to take the leap, established entrepreneurs looking for ways to grow a business, and those helping others start or grow a business (investors and coaches) to take three simple steps:

1. Take the Entrepreneurial StrengthsFinder assessment.

2. Become aware of their entrepreneurial talents and potential strengths and weaknesses.

3. Create a road map for future action.

Coaches, mentors, and city leaders: If you want to grow entrepreneurship in your communities and advise individuals about starting and growing businesses, you will be more effective once you understand the personality traits of those you mentor. Using the assessment, book, and guide, you can create a strengths-based development plan that will help aspiring or existing entrepreneurs use their natural talents to generate business outcomes. As a coach, you can also use the results of the talent assessment to help business partners understand each other's strengths and weaknesses and create productive partnerships.

Students and employees: If you are in the process of figuring out whether entrepreneurship is the right path for you or looking for ways to be more entrepreneurial in your current vocation, you can use the results from the assessment and book to become more agile in your thinking. Identifying your natural talents in the realm of entrepreneurship and nurturing an entrepreneurial mindset will greatly increase your likelihood of success at school or in your current job.

Entrepreneurs: If you are looking for insights into your behaviors that drive business outcomes, you can use this book as a guide to grow your business. Evaluating yourself on the 10 business-building traits, turning your innate talents into strengths, and identifying areas where you are likely to need help will increase your odds of success tremendously. In addition to knowing your unique talents, you can assess the talents of potential partners in your entrepreneurial journey.

Investors: If you are looking for the best candidates to bet on, you can use this book and the results of the assessment to pick the people with the highest likelihood of long-term success. Usually, investors base their decisions about candidates on a gut feeling. Augment that feeling or instincts — however much you trust them — with scientifically identified traits for successful business building. Use the results of this assessment to identify high-potential future founders and to support and encourage them to build successful companies.

Regardless of where you are on your life's journey, it is essential to identify and understand your entrepreneurial potential. Whether you are a coach, mentor, or city leader looking to create the next boom in your local economy or save your city from bankruptcy; a student considering starting a business; an employee looking to flex your entrepreneurial thinking in your job; an entrepreneur who is actively growing your business; or an investor looking to invest in the next best idea, I hope that this assessment, book, and guide will give you insight into how you can nurture your entrepreneurial talent to help you achieve your full potential.

THE 10 TALENTS OF SUCCESSFUL ENTREPRENEURS

BUSINESS FOCUS

CONFIDENCE

CREATIVE THINKER

DELEGATOR

DETERMINATION

INDEPENDENT

KNOWLEDGE-SEEKER

PROMOTER

RELATIONSHIP-BUILDER

RISK-TAKER

BUSINESS FOCUS

Key Traits:

- You are profit-oriented.

- You establish clear goals and objectively measure progress toward those goals.

- You judge the value of an opportunity, a relationship, or a decision by its effect on business.

- You invest time in planning growth strategies.

- You align employee responsibilities with company goals.

Highly successful entrepreneurs are fascinated by numbers and money. If you have high Business Focus, making money is your primary objective.

As an entrepreneur with high Business Focus, you have sharp business instincts, and you use them to price products or services to guarantee a profit on each sale. Consistent with your emphasis on money, you run a tight ship, keeping a close check on operational costs. You make all decisions, big and small, with cost in mind and evaluate your decisions through the prism of profitability. You constantly ask yourself, "How will this affect my bottom line?" Your focus on running the business efficiently makes you impatient with unnecessary costs caused by delays, detours, or obstacles.

Your attitude toward data reflects your penchant for numbers. Your high Business Focus gives you an uncanny ability to look at the same data that your managers, co-founders, or employees have reviewed and come up with unique insights that they may have missed. Numbers are your lifeline. From weekly target meetings to monthly tracks to quarterly company reviews, numbers are the topic of discussion. Not only do you relentlessly measure all aspects of the business, you know how each number is derived and what day-to-day team member actions affect these numbers.

As a business-focused entrepreneur, you also have a long-term view of the enterprise. With a futuristic outlook, you energize yourself and your team members by painting your vision of what the company will be like months and years from now — and you do it often. Even though monthly and quarterly scrutiny is important, you are focused on the long-term drivers of success and invest a lot of time planning for this future state. You set targets — financial and non-financial — for the month, quarter, year, and decade. Once you have set the targets, you innately understand what steps to take and what levers to pull to achieve them. Then you continuously monitor and measure the results, benchmarking them against the best in the industry. This gives you an objective view of how well the company is doing.

You don't stop with just setting and monitoring goals. You move on to the most critical step: getting your team on board and helping each team member understand how his or her daily actions drive the numbers. As a profit-oriented entrepreneur, you instinctively know how to align employee responsibilities with company goals by finding the right job fit for each employee. And you align each employee's responsibilities with his or her innate talents so each individual can bring his or her best self to the job every day.

A word of caution for entrepreneurs with high Business Focus: In your drive to maximize profits, you can sometimes lose sight of your customers. Remember to make customer orientation part of your business philosophy. Encourage your team to focus on increasing customer satisfaction along with the push to maximize revenues.

In addition, be cognizant of your team members' morale. A relentless focus on profitability and a competitive cost culture puts immense pressure on employees to maintain the highest levels of performance. Communicate your vision of the future clearly and often to keep the troops energized and morale high.

Along the same lines, never let your employees forget that you value their hard work. Recognizing them for their contributions, big and small, builds loyalty and commitment to the company, pushing them to perform at higher levels. Engaged employees' energy and effort will pull the company through tough times.

Business Focus in Action:

Warren Buffett, chairman and CEO of Berkshire Hathaway: "Whenever I read about some company undertaking a cost-cutting program, I know it's not a company that really knows what costs are all about. Spurts don't work in this area. The really good manager does not wake up in the morning and say, 'This is the day I'm going to cut costs,' any more than he wakes up and decides to practice breathing."

Larry Page, CEO of Google Inc.: "Our goal is long-term growth in revenue and absolute profit — so we invest aggressively in future innovation while tightly managing our short-term costs."

Bill Gates, business magnate, philanthropist, and inventor: "Warren (Buffett) and I have the most fun when we're taking the same data that everybody else has and coming up with new ways of looking at them that are both novel and, in a sense, obvious. Each of us tries to do this all the time for our respective companies, but it's particularly enjoyable and stimulating to discuss these insights with each other."

Maximizing Your Business Focus Talent:

1. *Use specific timelines and yardsticks to measure your business goals.* Applying precise measures will help you track the numbers and gauge how well your business is moving toward your goals.

2. *Manage your time carefully.* As an entrepreneur, there are many demands on your time. Make a list of well-defined initiatives that require your full attention. Reject proposals that don't further your business and financial goals.

3. *Write down your vision for the short term and long term, and refer to it often.* Putting your vision in writing and revisiting it regularly will keep you feeling in control and on track.

4. *Communicate your short-term and long-term goals consistently to your employees and clients.* Create a vivid road map for them to follow. Outline your strategies, and include examples, stories, action plans, and mock-ups. Help others see the future along with you. Your employees and customers must be able to see the company through your eyes. It will help them stay emotionally engaged. Work with them to define that future.

5. *Don't lose sight of the human element in business.* Your decisions and your extreme focus on profitability affect your employees and customers. Remember that you are working with people and not just spreadsheets and data.

6. *To help you set realistic business goals, learn everything you can about all aspects of your business.* Read trade journals, industry-specific publications, and technological breakthroughs related to your business. Talk to experts in your area.

CONFIDENCE

Key Traits:

- You know yourself and present yourself effectively with confidence.

- You clearly understand and can influence others.

- You are action-oriented and take initiative.

- You have conviction in your ability to be a successful entrepreneur.

Highly successful entrepreneurs have little self-doubt — rather, they are more likely to possess strong self-belief. If you have high Confidence, you believe that you have what it takes to be a successful entrepreneur.

Your certainty in your ability helps you start businesses, persist in the face of ambiguity and failure, and remain confident in meeting challenges as you pursue business success. You recognize opportunities and initiate action. While uncertainty may plague others — who endlessly weigh the potential value of an opportunity, gauge the complexities in the environment, and fall prey to "analysis paralysis" — a resilient self-belief leads you to act. And act quickly. You are so confident in your ability to control the events in your life and to manage your environment effectively that you know you will succeed. Your high Confidence also helps you convince others — investors, customers, prospective employees, and potential partners — of your ability to get positive results.

Entrepreneurs with high Confidence perform well in stressful conditions. You believe that bigger challenges bring greater rewards and that strong, persistent efforts will lead to success. You see little possibility for failure, choose courses of action that you think have a high probability of success, and avoid situations where you feel less in control. When others see risk, you see opportunity. When others see roadblocks and potential failure, you see victory.

What's more, as an entrepreneur with high Confidence, you like to build your knowledge base. The more information you have about a particular situation, the less risk you see in pursuing the opportunity. This gives you more confidence in your decisions and improves your likelihood of success.

Your certainty in your ideas and your ability to make things happen motivate you to create and commercialize new products and services. Your strong Confidence talents inspire continuous innovation that helps your company grow and survive.

Entrepreneurs with high Confidence assume that growth will continue well into the future. Indeed, you are quite focused on the long-term horizon, driven by your unshakeable belief in your ability to build large, successful enterprises. You are willing to navigate the difficulties of a business cycle, gradually accumulating human and financial resources, constantly investing in new ideas, expanding the company's knowledge base, and attracting better talent to ensure your long-term success. You take your responsibility to steward the company into the future very seriously.

A word of caution: Entrepreneurial confidence and conviction grows businesses, but *overconfidence* can be harmful to an enterprise's health. Sometimes overconfident entrepreneurs make decisions in haste, underestimating the complexity of the situation. You can avoid jeopardizing your company's future by slowing down and considering all the relevant factors before making a decision. This is especially true if your business is in a dynamic industry with a complex environment and a constantly changing landscape.

At times, you can underestimate the resources required for company survival or growth by overestimating your ability to get results with minimal staff, materials, and equipment. At other times, you overcommit resources in pursuit of a certain idea or opportunity without assessing the competition and market readiness. This is especially true when entering new and untested markets.

What's more, if you are an early mover into a business sector, you should pay close attention to customer needs and readiness, technological issues, supply chain contingencies, and delivery systems you need to bring the product or service to the market. Paying heed to these issues will prevent you from making mistakes and wasting money and resources — and will increase the likelihood of your company's survival and growth.

Confidence in Action:

Warren Buffett: "I always knew I was going to be rich. I don't think I ever doubted it for a minute."

Michael Dell, CEO and chairman of Dell, Inc., when asked, at age 19, what he wanted to do with his life, told his dad: "Compete with IBM."

Malcolm Gladwell, author of *The Tipping Point* and *Blink*, explaining overconfidence: "As novices, we don't trust our judgment. Then we have some success, and begin to feel a little surer of ourselves. Finally, we get to the top of our game and succumb to the trap of thinking that there's nothing we can't master. As we get older and more experienced, we overestimate the accuracy of our judgments, especially when the task before us is difficult and when we're involved with something of great personal importance."

Maximizing Your Confidence Talent:

1. *Plan ahead to boost your confidence.* Draw an elaborate business plan with rich details. Project multiple scenarios, run analysis, and outline resource needs before taking action. Set milestones and outcome expectations for each stage of a project. Prepare for contingencies. While you are already confident in your ability to be successful, thorough planning can validate and support your certainty and help you achieve your objectives.

2. *Do your homework.* To make your product or service ready for the market, collect as much information as you can about industry specifications, procedures and documents, competitors, value proposition to customers, intellectual property protection issues, and technological requirements.

3. *Avoid the "speed trap."* Don't let your strong sense of self-belief and initiative push you to make decisions under pressure. When the window of opportunity is narrow and you have to make decisions quickly, pause to reinforce your certainty by considering your experiences, knowledge, and what-if scenarios before you take action.

4. *Discuss opportunities with your network.* Consider your self-image in these discussions. You are sure of yourself and easily influence others. But your network ties can help you assess opportunities in a different light. Listen to their points of view to get a more complete picture of the situation. They can also help you access resources to pursue those opportunities.

5. *Avoid "in-group" thinking.* Your self-confidence and strong desire for control may cause you to surround yourself with people who are not likely to challenge your thinking. Seek feedback from diverse stakeholders — managers, senior executives, board members, and investors. Their alternative outlooks on risks and opportunities will stimulate your sound decision making.

CREATIVE THINKER

Key Traits:

- You imagine beyond the boundaries of what exists now.

- You explore options and can think your way through problems.

- You constantly dream up new products or services for customers.

- You have a mind that is typically firing with many different ideas.

- You are a curious and quick learner.

Highly successful entrepreneurs can creatively look beyond the present and imagine possible futures for their company. If you are a Creative Thinker, you are driven to steer your business in new directions.

Whether introducing new products and services, entering untapped markets, or initiating innovative technologies or production processes, you are constantly thinking of novel ways to propel your business forward. Comfortable with the unknown and the unfamiliar, you always look for new ways to combine and recombine resources to create innovative solutions for your customers. Your creative action helps you renew your business' value proposition and differentiate it from your competitors'. It also enables you to disrupt markets by introducing new and unexpected products or by developing novel methods of doing business.

Creative Thinkers are alert to changes in the external business environment — new technologies, shifts in customer needs, industry trends, or competitor actions. You constantly evaluate new possibilities, revise your expectations of the imagined future, and formulate fresh action plans to achieve your goals. This endless cycle of new information, new opportunities, and new action plans helps you start ventures or grow existing ones.

As a Creative Thinker, you are quick to act. You seize opportunities and are usually the first mover in the market. Your unique ability to take an idea and quickly transform it into a business that generates revenue helps you stay ahead of the competition. And your proactivity garners your business high profits, allowing you to establish your brand and capture market share ahead of others in the industry

Highly creative entrepreneurs are rule breakers who don't like to conform to norms and traditions of the industry. You refuse to be bogged down by established practices, bureaucratic structures, or arcane business processes. You like to work autonomously, outside the established organizational practices, where you can think and create freely.

You constantly push the boundaries, always experimenting with new ideas to sort the good from the bad. It is this ability to experiment, usually in the face of acute uncertainty, that gives you the potential to generate innovative paths to profits.

A word of caution: While highly creative entrepreneurs are independent spirits who like to work autonomously, implementing ideas requires working with a team. Lack of communication with your team or too much separation from ongoing operations can hurt the development and integration of new products or services into an existing business. Make sure to communicate your ideas and strategies to your team. Sharing will increase the likelihood of launching a successful product or service.

In addition, you may fall prey to "incumbent inertia" as you achieve success and grow. Don't become complacent with growth. Maintain the organizational flexibility that allowed you to explore your creative imagination in the first place. Continue to pay attention to changing customer needs, evolving technologies, and the shifting business environment. Remember, this endless stream of new information and knowledge will fuel your creativity.

Be careful not to rush to launch new initiatives. Your creative tendency might cause you to experiment and launch multiple initiatives at the same time. This perceived lack of focus may hamper your chances of success. Don't lose sight of your core business.

Creative Thinker in Action:

Jeff Bezos, founder and CEO of Amazon.com: "If you double the number of experiments you do per year, you're going to double your inventiveness. The thing about inventing is you have to be both stubborn and flexible, more or less simultaneously. If you're not stubborn, you'll give up on experiments too soon. And if you're not flexible, you'll pound your head against the wall and you won't see a different solution to a problem you're trying to solve."

Marissa Mayer, president and CEO of Yahoo and former vice president of search products at Google: "The 'Googly' thing is to launch it [a product] early on Google Labs and then iterate, learning what the market wants — and making it great. The beauty of experimenting in this way is that you never get too far from what the market wants. The market pulls you back."

James Dyson, founder of Dyson: "We are all looking for the magic formula. Well, here you go: Creativity + Iterative Development = Innovation."

Maximizing Your Creative Thinker Talent:

1. *Balance current and future customer needs.* It is easy to be tied down with day-to-day business management and focused on delivering what your customers expect from you. Set aside time to disconnect from the present, and feed your creativity to imagine your customers' future needs. This will help you dream and plan for the future and maintain your competitive advantage.

2. *Use measurement to evaluate your ideas.* When weighing which idea to implement, ask yourself, "How can we measure this?" Pick ideas apart to identify issues that could crop up during implementation. If the results show that a project isn't viable, then modify

or abandon the idea and move on to the
next one.

3. *Minimize potential pitfalls by releasing
   your new product or service incrementally.*
   Implementing new ideas is risky. Iteration is
   key. Launch the prototype, gather feedback
   from customers, make necessary changes,
   and test again. Using this low-cost approach,
   you can turn your novel and creative ideas
   into products or services without much
   potential downside.

4. *Maintain a simple organizational structure.*
   Fewer layers of hierarchy will enable easier
   information flow between you and your
   team. A simple organizational structure
   will also increase employee involvement in
   implementing ideas, encourage employees'
   creativity, and lead to quicker execution and
   understanding of new ideas.

5. *Balance efficiency with creativity.* Process management techniques, such as total quality management or Six Sigma, which can increase your growing company's efficiency and productivity, are also likely to decrease your ability to innovate. Don't let efficiency-enhancing practices act as barriers to exploring new ideas. Nurture your natural creativity. Continue to invest in new ideas as you increase operational efficiency.

6. *Mobilize resources to fuel the innovation process.* You need two things for successful innovation: diverse experiences that spark your creativity and resources to drive the innovation process. Tap in to your existing network or build new alliances internally and externally to stimulate your creativity and access shared resources.

7. *Learn from your failures.* When carefully planned new initiatives fail, the potential to learn from them is immense. Don't let this learning opportunity go to waste. Conduct a post-mortem, make sense of what happened, and add what you have learned to your knowledge base. Fostering *intelligent failures* will help you learn what not to do as you dream about the future.

DELEGATOR

Key Traits:

- You readily delegate authority and responsibility.

- You proactively collaborate with others.

- You recognize and draw on people's special abilities.

- You help ensure that team members become effective contributors.

Highly successful entrepreneurs quickly adjust to accommodate the changing needs and new realities of a growing business. If you are a Delegator, you understand that a rapidly growing venture needs capabilities and resources beyond what you alone can provide.

Delegators work *on* the business rather than *in* it. You recognize that a growing business requires a shift from a do-it-yourself style, which is helpful in the early stages, to a more hands-off approach as the business starts to grow. You are well aware that you cannot possibly accomplish everything yourself, and you are willing to relinquish control and hand off authority for certain tasks to others who are better equipped to handle them. You have mastered the art of delegation. This frees up your time to focus on activities that yield the highest returns for the company and that grow the business.

You develop team capacity and delegate wisely. You understand your employees' capabilities and strengths and position them to take responsibility for tasks at which they are most likely to excel. You also give employees autonomy to make decisions related to their tasks, which fosters psychological ownership and engagement. Engaged and motivated employees are more likely to take initiative to build better systems and streamline work processes, thus increasing productivity and benefitting the company.

Simply put, effective Delegators are great managers and supportive bosses. You set clear expectations about timing, budget, and deliverables; make sure employees have the tools and resources they need to do their jobs; provide opportunities for training and learning; and genuinely care about the growth of each individual. You seek input from your employees and value their opinions and expertise.

What's more, you encourage new ideas and approaches to getting things done, and you are focused on outcomes rather than processes. You recognize employees for a job well done, thus creating an atmosphere of mutual respect and trust. Effective delegation increases employee commitment, boosts morale, and positively influences company performance.

A word of caution: While you do delegate effectively, *do not abdicate* your overall responsibility for a project. The buck stops with you. Remember to set milestones to monitor progress, and communicate frequently with the people to whom you are delegating to avoid costly mistakes or surprises. When they complete tasks, provide feedback about what worked and what didn't. Set up a successful delegation process. In the long run, it will build employee capacity and, more importantly, save you time — time you can use to create new opportunities for your business.

Delegator in Action:

Carol Loomis, a *Fortune* editor-at-large, on Warren Buffett: "As long as numbers are looking as they should, though, Buffett does not poke into operations, but rather leaves his managers free to run their businesses as their intelligence tells them to."

Charlie Munger, vice chairman of Berkshire Hathaway: "We chose our style of operation to fit our natures, which demanded that plenty of time be spent thinking and learning. Naturally, this caused extreme delegation. Warren [Buffett] and I avoid doing anything that someone else at Berkshire can do better."

Scott Heiferman, CEO of Meetup.com: "Avoid thinking that you have to do it all. Divide and conquer. Do what you are best at and let others take care of the rest. Each founder should focus on his or her strengths."

Maximizing Your Delegator Talent:

1. *Identify what to delegate.* Make a detailed list of all the activities on your plate. Ask yourself two questions as you go through the list: 1. Is this activity critical for the growth of my business? 2. Is there someone else who can do it better? Strategic planning, managing important customer relationships, hiring decisions, and confidential tasks are critical duties that usually require your direct attention. On the other hand, for accounting, legal work, social media, IT functions, and administrative tasks, there is usually someone else who can do it better, so delegate.

2. *Identify whom to delegate to.* If you have hired people with the right talents and skills, then it will be easy for you to identify the right person for each task. Match the job to the individual with the appropriate expertise to deliver results, not just to those who aren't busy.

3. *Take time to set things up for success.* One of the main hurdles to delegation is the amount of time it takes to train someone. It is worth your time to make sure employees have what they need to do the job right. Give others clear instructions and enough time to complete tasks.

4. *Allow employees to perform.* Be patient. Manage the process by focusing on the results. Set clear milestones for key stages of the project, and monitor progress.

5. *Give feedback.* Effective delegation builds the capacity of your team. Talk to employees about what works and what does not. As they learn to fine-tune their actions, they will improve their performance on each task and be able to take on more responsibility.

6. *Use your network to access the human resources you need for delegation.* If hiring new employees is not an option, borrow or barter resources to keep costs in check.

DETERMINATION

Key Traits:

- You push to achieve and have a tremendous work ethic.

- You confront obstacles directly and overcome them.

- You are persistent and undeterred by failures or roadblocks.

- You are eager to make decisions and quick to act.

Highly successful entrepreneurs have a high *adversity quotient* — the ability to recover from setbacks. If you have high Determination, you believe you have the ability to confront and overcome insurmountable obstacles.

Entrepreneurs with high Determination don't give up when the going gets tough. Delays and obstructions don't deter you. Your tenacity and persistence allow you to recover from setbacks and failures. Whether confronted by a failed project, an unsuccessful product launch, or a disastrous end to a new venture, you know how to pick yourself up and resume your efforts. You strongly believe that you can overcome any obstacle by working harder.

You believe you have the capacity to control your circumstances, and you are highly motivated to change adversity into opportunity by taking action. Instead of giving in to feelings of frustration and anger, when you encounter obstacles, you can see beyond the roadblocks and visualize a better future. Your optimistic attitude helps you attain the desired business outcome.

You take personal accountability for the consequences of your choices and actions, and doing so mobilizes you to act. You strongly believe that your setbacks and failures are the result of a lack of effort on your part, and you are willing to do whatever it takes to fix things. This compels you to double your efforts, try new options, and push forward when faced with adversity.

Entrepreneurs with high Determination tenaciously pursue goals. You identify opportunities, take initiative, and persevere when faced with obstacles. You are focused on winning and will not take no for an answer. This attitude helps you launch new businesses, enter new markets, and invent new products despite formidable barriers.

Further, you have a high tolerance for stress and an immense capacity for sustained hard work. You confront every situation with robust energy and stamina; setbacks and obstacles strengthen your resolve to remain on task and work harder. Your ability to put in long hours ensures that your business survives through numerous ups and downs.

A word of caution: Entrepreneurs with high tenacity and perseverance can have a misplaced commitment to a selected course of action. In other words, you may have a tendency to stick with a failing strategy or continue allocating resources to a pet project or product, even when the results are consistently below expectations. You are also likely to harbor deep discontent, disappointment, and regret when faced with a failing venture or an unsuccessful launch. Because you have extremely high expectations for success, are highly dedicated, and are completely vested in your business, any outcome that doesn't meet your expectations can trigger regretful thinking.

In addition, you routinely make tough calls in the course of running your business — for instance, firing employees, litigating with competitors to protect intellectual property, negotiating late payments with financiers, or sorting disputes with suppliers. Having to make unpleasant decisions comes at a great personal cost to the highly vested entrepreneur. Understand that despite your extreme commitment to your venture, you might not attain all of your business goals. Keep close tabs on business outcomes, and adjust your strategy if necessary.

Determination in Action:

Thomas Edison, American inventor and businessman: "I have not failed. I've just found 10,000 ways that won't work."

Richard Branson, founder of Virgin: "If you are hurt, lick your wounds and get up again. If you've given it your absolute best, it's time to move forward."

Wang Chuan-Fu, founder and CEO of BYD, the Chinese electric car and battery company, when asked by Warren Buffett how BYD would sustain its lead in the market: "We'll never, never rest."

Maximizing Your Determination Talent:

1. *Share your optimistic outlook with your partners, employees, and investors.* You see possibilities where others see barriers. Your determined optimism and work ethic will inspire and energize your team to do more.

2. *Energize your Determination talent by partnering with creative individuals.* Working with inventive people can inspire you. Your uncanny ability to sort through many ideas and hone in on the best one will help transform their idea into a product or service for a customer.

3. *Always keep the big picture of your business in mind.* This will help you navigate your way through the twists and turns of the entrepreneurial journey and strengthen your natural tendency to push forward in adverse circumstances.

4. *Monitor your progress toward predefined goals.* When executing a strategy, set specific milestones so you know if the strategy is working or if you need to change course. This way, you can avoid costly mistakes early.

5. *Be attentive to the constantly shifting business landscape.* Your tenacity to see a pet project or product through may blind you to changes in the market. Pay close attention to new technologies, a changing customer base, and emerging new business models. Staying aware of your business environment will help you switch gears if necessary.

6. *Don't focus on the cause of setbacks.* Rather, direct your energy toward activities that can help you move forward. Setbacks and challenges are part of the entrepreneurial journey. Improving your reaction to adverse circumstances will keep you upbeat and reduce downtime when you do encounter obstacles.

7. *Keep things in perspective.* Making tough calls is part of running a business. Don't dwell on unpleasant decisions. Rely on your support system — business partners, investors, mentors, and family members — to help you deal with the personal toll these decisions can take on you.

8. *Reflect on your successes and failures.* Set aside time to analyze why a decision yielded positive or negative results. Replicate the positive, and weed out the actions or behaviors that produced negative outcomes. Over time, you will build a repertoire of skills to make effective business decisions.

INDEPENDENT

Key Traits:

- You depend on yourself to get the job done.

- You have a strong sense of responsibility.

- You can handle multiple tasks successfully.

- You are resolute, with a high level of competence in every aspect of managing a business.

Highly successful entrepreneurs strongly believe they can take an idea from concept to creation based on their efforts alone. If you have high Independent talent, you consider yourself a jack-of-all-trades who can single-handedly start and operate a business.

Independent entrepreneurs like to launch ventures. Your ability to multitask and your extremely strong sense of responsibility help you tackle the basics of starting a business on your own. From recognizing opportunities to gathering resources to building networks to setting goals to implementing strategies, you can do it all. Your self-reliance greatly increases an early-stage business' odds of survival.

As an Independent entrepreneur, you autonomously set goals and take action to achieve them. You have high expectations of success that push you to develop specific strategies to attain your desired outcomes. You firmly believe that your actions decide the fate of your business. Consequently, you are motivated to make things happen. Your can-do attitude explains your early entrepreneurial success.

You actively access tangible resources — real estate, workspace, communication infrastructure, or marketing materials — as well as intangible ones — brand name, technological capability, organizational processes, customer relationships, or company culture — to start and grow a new venture. And to ensure the venture operates efficiently and effectively, you proficiently develop strategies to maximize all these resources.

You are extremely committed to your business. Starting an enterprise is a grueling process, and your reserves of high energy and a vast capacity for hard work enable you to make it happen. Your wholehearted dedication to your new business ensures its survival and success.

Dealing with the unknown and uncertain energizes you. Early-stage businesses are rife with ambiguity and day-to-day challenges. Your ability to think and act quickly allows you to develop creative solutions to complex problems. Your agile mind can quickly make modifications to your business plan, product or service mix, customer base, resource needs, and implementation strategies as needed.

A word of caution: Independence is critical in the startup phase as you translate an idea into an operational business with minimal help. But, as the venture begins to flourish, the desire for complete autonomy and control over every aspect of the business can hinder its growth. Go-it-alone entrepreneurs can get things done, but that trait can keep you from focusing on activities that bring the highest value to a growing business. In addition, 20-hour days packed with multiple tasks could lead to burnout, jeopardizing the very survival of the venture.

As your business grows, it is impossible to do everything yourself. Develop processes and systems to handle repetitive tasks. Hire, train, and then transfer certain responsibilities to your staff. Keep checks in place to ensure things are on track. Having the right people and processes in place will keep you in control of your business without personally handling every task.

Independent in Action:

Mona Simpson about her brother, Steve Jobs (1955-2011), co-founder, chairman, and CEO of Apple: "He was never embarrassed about working hard, even if the results were failures."

Sachin Kamdar, CEO of Parse.ly: "The role of a CEO almost changes every single month as your company grows ... one day you could find yourself being an account manager, the next day you're a salesperson, the next day you're HR and recruiting, the next day you're a marketer. It's honestly been a challenge to deal with all these different things you have to as CEO of the company and trying to manage yourself and your time."

Chad Hurley, co-founder of YouTube: "As you start building the product, don't assume that you know all the answers. Be prepared to adapt. You may have initial thoughts or ideas on how something will work but you need to observe how you and the community are using it. Don't be afraid to change direction midcourse."

Maximizing Your Independent Talent:

1. *Plan for the long term.* Your complete focus on the here and now will ensure the survival of your venture. But make sure

your short-term goals align with your long-term objectives for the ultimate success and longevity of your company.

2. *Don't lose sight of your main objective.* Set clear criteria to make sure you are on the right track in the early stages of your venture. It is easy to get lost in the day-to-day minutiae. Stay focused on the reason you started the venture in the first place.

3. *Be prepared to "pivot" quickly.* Pay attention to your competition, customer segment, technology, business regulations, and the business environment. The more you know, the quicker you'll be able to adapt to changing circumstances.

4. *Form strategic alliances and a diverse network.* While you have a natural tendency to be autonomous, connections can help you secure resources in the early stages of your business — resources you may not have

direct ownership of or access to. In addition, a diverse network increases the likelihood of you reaching a broader audience for your new products or services.

5. *Don't develop entrepreneurial myopia.* Resist falling in love with your idea or product. Try to be objective about the product or service you want to offer to the market. Assess the market need, be aware of the competition, and understand your target customer. Develop a product or service that aligns with your customers' needs.

6. *Hire staff members who can meet the needs of your growing business.* As your business expands and your offerings in the market diversify, realize that you will have to delegate. Be sure to hire employees who have talents and skills that fit your organization. This will free you up to work on things that grow your business.

KNOWLEDGE-SEEKER

Key Traits:

- You push yourself to acquire in-depth information about every aspect of your business.

- You use knowledge as a competitive advantage.

- You have a preoccupation with your business that borders on obsession.

- You anticipate knowledge needs and use knowledge well.

Highly successful entrepreneurs are obsessed with their business; they have a strong desire to acquire in-depth knowledge about all aspects of it. If you are a Knowledge-Seeker, you constantly search for new information and experiences to navigate your company in a highly complex business environment.

Starting and growing a venture is a formidable task. The demands on the entrepreneur are many:

mapping the industry landscape, understanding what products and services to offer, raising capital, managing employees and customers, and competing in a global economy. You inherently understand that *knowledge* is a valuable asset. You use your vast knowledge to analyze complex business environments, solve problems, select the best course of action, and stay ahead of the competition.

As a Knowledge-Seeker, you plumb your deep reservoirs of learning to enter new markets and to compete more effectively in the existing market. You gather an incredible amount of information and store every new fact, fresh piece of data, and new experience in your mental library, constantly asking yourself, "What does this mean for my business?" This accumulation of knowledge greatly increases your chances of finding and exploiting discoveries that others may miss.

What's more, you can foresee the utility of products or services that the market is not yet expecting. Just as Henry Ford upended the transportation market by introducing the mass-produced automobile and Steve Jobs' iPad disrupted the traditional PC market, you systematically apply knowledge to innovate disruptively.

You also use your encyclopedic knowledge to keep competition at bay, which helps you gain precious market share and maintain continued profitability. For instance, you might learn about intellectual property law to guard against competitors imitating your discoveries. Similarly, you strive to obtain information about new production processes, technologies, bundling of services, or business models to give you a competitive advantage.

Knowledge-Seekers assess and manage risk effectively. Entrepreneurs have to make decisions in highly complex environments with incomplete information, which entails much risk. Your ability to collect and process a lot of information gives you a better understanding of your environment. Whether you have to make a decision about releasing a new product or service, rolling out a new marketing strategy, or introducing a new production process, you understand the implications of the choices you face, calculate the inherent risk in each, and select the best course of action.

You have a superior insight into your customers' needs. Constantly driven to gather knowledge about the business environment, you quickly recognize trends in consumer behavior and effectively reallocate organizational resources to cater to changing customer expectations. This behavior turns your customers into advocates and generates higher revenue.

In short, Knowledge-Seekers never stop learning. Your ability to absorb knowledge and information gives your company a much higher chance of survival and growth.

A word of caution: As a Knowledge-Seeker, your intellectual curiosity may generate *too many* new ideas and insights. You might pivot from one idea to the next — sometimes too quickly — confusing your employees and customers. This can hamper day-to-day decision making as teams grapple with constant change in direction and incoherent strategy.

Knowing how to differentiate between ideas that truly improve your business from those that do not is the key. Select ideas that streamline your business and add value for your customers. Avoid the lure of implementing every idea and insight without measured reflection.

Knowledge-Seeker in Action:

Paul B. Allen, founder of Ancestry.com: "I devoured every article and news release and case study I could find on dot-com companies. I believe I read cover to cover nearly every issue of *The Industry Standard*, *Red Herring*, *Business 2.0*, *Wired*, *Upside*, and several other Internet publications. I scoured dozens of reports from Jupiter Communications and from leading stock market analysts. I attended dozens of industry conferences and events. And I filtered all the information and ideas I learned about through a simple lens: 'How would this work in genealogy and with families?' It was our ability and insatiable desire to learn and experiment in a fast-moving environment that made us the world leader in online genealogy."

Michael Goldberg, president of Berkshire Hathaway Credit Corp., on Warren Buffett: "He is constantly examining all that he hears: 'Is it consistent and plausible? Is it wrong?' He has a model in his head of the whole world. The computer there compares every new fact with all that he's ever experienced and knows about — and says, 'What does this mean for us?' For Berkshire, that is."

Thane Stenner, founder of Stenner Investment Partners, on successful entrepreneurs: "There always seems to be a common thread amongst this uncommonly well-to-do subset. They all have a different story, a different path. However, what is a common trait in virtually all of them is that they are 'intellectually curious.' They love to learn. They look for insights, always a better way of doing things ... an 'edge.'"

Maximizing Your Knowledge-Seeker Talent:

1. *Feed your voracious desire to know everything related to your business.* Read new material on industry-specific websites; in trade publications, annual reports, and newsletters; and on social media. Write and share ideas and insights with others, and brainstorm with those inside and outside the company. Learning everything you can will help you cultivate expertise in different aspects of your business.

2. *Set aside plenty of time for thinking and learning.* Delegate tasks to others. Free up your time from the daily minutiae to focus on things that help grow your business.

3. *Sort through your insights before initiating action.* Your vast knowledge base generates many ideas. Focus on the truly important and meaningful ones that will move your business forward.

4. *Get an outsider's point of view.* Your immense depth of knowledge makes you confident in the viability of your ideas. Consider sharing your insights with someone who can challenge your assumptions and provide feedback on the feasibility of your ideas.

5. *Give your employees clear direction.* Your considerable intellectual ability might lead you to change the direction of your business rapidly. Constant change can confuse your employees. Create a road map they can follow.

PROMOTER

Key Traits:

- You speak boldly on behalf of your company.

- You can make your case effectively and influence people.

- You communicate your vision of your company to employees and customers.

- You have a clear growth strategy.

Highly successful entrepreneurs are ambassadors who represent the interests of their company to the outside world. If you are a Promoter, you are the face and voice of your company, and you champion your enterprise and endorse what it stands for at every opportunity.

As a Promoter, you are an excellent communicator who instinctively knows how to reach your audience. Incredibly persuasive, you are a great salesperson who can influence others to accept your point of view. Your open and authentic behavior helps you forge trusting relationships with investors, customers, partners, and employees that help you launch new products and services to grow your business.

Promoters are exceptional storytellers. You communicate the essence of your company, your idea, or your new product or service through stories that reflect your personal experiences. You create an emotional connection with the audience by sharing your passion and excitement about the product or service, but also by speaking to your listeners' needs. Your storytelling helps rally support for your cause from your partners and customers and furthers your business goals.

Promoters have outstanding sales talent. As an attentive listener, you are quick to assess customer needs and can clearly and compellingly articulate how your product or service will meet those needs. Your unbridled enthusiasm and deep conviction in your product or service inspires trust and persuades your prospects to say yes. You establish your credibility by being forthright and sharing facts. This reassures your clients and fosters long-term customer commitment.

You instinctively know how to invest in people and relationships that are beneficial to your business. You form close connections with employees so they feel emotionally invested in their work, with investors or donors to secure financial resources you need to grow, with vendors who get emotionally attached to your product, and with customers to turn them into evangelists. You can cultivate a community of supporters who become the ambassadors for your products or services.

A word of caution: Highly successful Promoters have a natural tendency to believe that their company, product, or service has the potential to change the world. Your closeness to your idea or product and an intense desire to see it succeed may blind you to its flaws. While storytelling and advocacy are critical to growing a business, be objective about the product or service you promote. Surround yourself with trusted advisers who will help you assess situations and scenarios objectively. Take the time to build something that will truly solve someone's problem. Promoting a solid product or service builds customer trust and long-term commitment.

In addition, even though you like to be the face of your company, consider if that is in the enterprise's best interest. Sure, when an entrepreneur writes syndicated columns or blogs, appears in the media, and gives speeches, it can give a business a distinct identity and help it grow. But creating a single dominant persona that represents the company may be counterproductive for businesses that need to emphasize the availability of diverse expert resources for the customer. And the reality is, a company that is built around the personality of its founder or owner may find it hard to convince customers to work with anyone else, potentially restricting its growth. Sometimes, it is better to present multiple faces and voices of your company.

Promoter in Action:

David Ogilvy, founder of Ogilvy & Mather and known as "The Father of Advertising": "In the modern world of business, it is useless to be a creative, original thinker unless you can also sell what you create."

Peter Guber, chairman and CEO of Mandalay Entertainment Group: "My experience at Sony demonstrated that the face-to-face telling of the right story in the right room at the right time and in the right way can galvanize listeners to action and reset the teller's success trajectory."

Dino Bernacchi, Harley-Davidson's director of North American marketing operations, explaining the company's customer-led approach to marketing: "*United by Independents* is as much a rally cry to discover your ultimate self-expression and personal freedom as it is a celebration of fans and riders that continue to defy stereotypes of what it means to be a Harley-Davidson enthusiast. The campaign is cast entirely through social media with real riders from across the globe and from all walks of life who are united by their shared passion for the brand and their love of riding."

Maximizing Your Promoter Talent:

1. *Build a great product or service.* Make sure to anticipate your customers' needs as you create your product or service. Shrewdly designed products and services empower customers and are easy to build a brand around and easy to promote.

2. *Be the expert.* Position yourself as the expert on your company's products and services. Blog, speak, and write about the value they bring to your customers. Use your natural storytelling talent to elaborate on how your products or services are different from the sea of competition out there. The information you offer will establish you as the expert your customers can trust.

3. *Rehearse your story.* Take every opportunity to practice your storytelling technique. Refine your story based on your audience's feedback. Go beyond your personal experiences and add anecdotes from history, mythology, politics, and literature. Create a message that helps you achieve your organization's goals.

4. *Use multiple media to reach the widest audience possible.* In addition to traditional means of communication, make the most of media such as Twitter, Facebook, texting, and blogging. The more accessible you are, the more seeds you plant.

5. *Build and support a community for your products and services.* Your company can benefit greatly from customers who love your product or service. Identify them, and help them champion your offerings. Provide them with the latest information on the product or service, give them a forum to share their

views, use their feedback to improve your product or service, share their stories on your company website, and give them physical space to hold meetings and interact with your employees. In short, help create a community of evangelists for your company.

RELATIONSHIP-BUILDER

Key Traits:

- You have high social awareness.

- You attract and maintain a constituency.

- You build mutually beneficial relationships.

- You use your relationship talents to access internal and external resources.

- You forge relationships with employees and customers that go beyond work.

- You have an open demeanor, positive attitude, and personal integrity that help build trust.

Highly successful entrepreneurs have strong interpersonal skills that allow them to build a robust and diversified personal network. If you are a Relationship-Builder, you inherently understand that running a successful company is a collective effort that requires interaction with a range of people: suppliers and potential investors, employees and customers, peers, competitors, public officials, and members of the media.

A Relationship-Builder's approach is twofold: You use your social ties to access critical resources (financial and non-financial) for your business. And you use your networks to: gain information, share experiences, exchange ideas, pool expertise, draw mutual support, and help sustain motivation, thus increasing the likelihood of your venture's survival and success.

You instinctively know how to respond to and engage with customers, employees, and suppliers who are critical to your success. Using personalized interactions, an ability to accurately perceive customer needs, and an accessible attitude, you generate trust and confidence in your brand. You make sure that you retain your best customers, and thus the market share, by creating an emotional bond with them.

Similarly, Relationship-Builders create workplaces with a shared sense of purpose that connects employees on an emotional level. Your optimism and high personal integrity help build trust and loyalty with employees, motivating them to give more of themselves to their role.

Your social competence also helps you form mutually trusting relationships with your suppliers. These connections encourage both parties to go beyond contractual obligations and result in long-term relationships. You consider your suppliers to be partners, and you invest equity *and* trust in them. You maintain these lasting relationships with your partners by giving them clear requirements for products or services you need, aggressive cost-reduction targets, and competitive pricing — and by demonstrating a willingness to share risk in case of unforeseen events.

Your authenticity and confidence in what you know help you secure financial resources for your company. You can clearly articulate the future state of your business and the resources you need to bring your ideas to fruition. Investors respond to this confidence and integrity. People in your network are willing to do more for you than is expected of them.

Your high social competence also allows you to extract information from your networks. You know what you can get, from whom, and when. You share experiences, exchange ideas, and make new contacts with people inside and outside your industry. These interactions help you discover new technologies, markets, and processes and may result in new partnership opportunities — all essential for the growth of your business.

The breadth and depth of your networks empower you to confidently and aggressively take risks, try something new, and bear losses and failures. Failure can be extremely painful for you, both financially and psychologically. But your strong and diversified network is a source of emotional support and builds your confidence in times of loss or failure. Your network is a social safety net that can soften the pain and cost of entrepreneurial failure, help diminish feelings of isolation, and provide inspiration for fresh business ideas.

A word of caution for the Relationship-Builder: The very ties that help grow businesses can sometimes hamper growth. Three things to be wary about:

1. Bigger is not always better. Highly successful entrepreneurs don't necessarily have larger networks. Be selective about the associations you form. Your confidence in knowing what to expect from whom, and how to get it, helps you garner resources for your venture.

2. Overinvestment in your network may take precious time away from focusing on your business. Invest your time wisely.

3. Sometimes strong networks can shut out new people and new thinking, insulating you from fresh input from the "outside." Just as real capital becomes less productive with age, your social capital can become old

and stagnant. It needs regular maintenance and investment. Changing business needs will require you to retain the ties that work, abolish those that become obsolete or non-productive, and forge new ones. Remember, introducing new elements into your network will generate new experiences and positive change.

Relationship-Builder in Action:

Roy Spence, chairman, CEO, and co-founder of marketing communications and advertising company GSD&M: "The key to long-term meaningful, and yes happy and fun, success is to create partnerships of purpose with people you like and who like you. I never did understand the idea of 'don't do business with your friends.' I love building relationships with people who love building something special and making money by making a difference."

David Bradford, lawyer turned tech guru and serial entrepreneur: "I can't think of anything more fun than connecting people. People make businesses happen. It's that simple."

Maximizing Your Relationship-Builder Talent:

1. *Diversify your networks.* Go beyond your *vertical* ties (people in your immediate circle and those you know well) to cultivate *horizontal* (your competitors, customers, and suppliers) and *lateral* ties (entrepreneurs from unrelated businesses and people outside the business world such as media personnel and government officials).

2. *Remember that reciprocity is vital to maintaining strong relationships.* Offer help, connect people with each other, or share industry information. Others will respond when you need help.

3. *Be selective in whom you invest the most time.* Spend time with your most important customers, your most productive employees, and those who can make the most difference to your business. These relationships will render returns in the immediate future and in the long term.

4. *Understand the local social landscape.* Pay attention to the existing bonds, loyalties, and networks that characterize the community in which you work and live. Recognize the norms, values, and preferences that shape the behavior of other entrepreneurs and non-entrepreneurs in your community. This will help you form a durable and effective network that you can maximize for your business interests.

5. *Use your time, brand, and resources to address social issues.* Build a constituency — a collection of people who have shared beliefs, interests, and ambitions. Remember that your customers and employees are part of your community. Collaborating with them on solving social problems will turn them into engaged advocates of your business and your most powerful allies.

6. *Renew and reshape your networks frequently.* Place people who are critical for your business and who you keep in touch with in your *active network*. Nurture these relationships carefully. Put contacts whose usefulness has diminished over time into your *inactive network*. Prune this list aggressively and often. Your *potential network* is a list of new connections vital to the future of your business. Figure out strategies to build these connections.

RISK-TAKER

Key Traits:

- You have a strong personality, charisma, and confidence.

- You are enthusiastic when taking on challenges.

- You have a highly optimistic perception of risk.

- You make decisions easily in complex situations.

- You take a rational approach to decision making.

Contrary to popular belief, highly successful entrepreneurs are not risk seekers, they are risk *mitigators* par excellence. If you are a Risk-Taker, you instinctively know how to manage high-risk situations.

When encountering a challenging decision, you take an analytical approach, meticulously gathering as much information as you can, weighing all the options, and assessing everything that can possibly go wrong. Replacing emotion with a rational thought process helps you overcome fear, calculate your odds of success, and then decide whether to assume risks, such as committing resources to new projects, introducing new products and services, entering new markets, or investing in new technologies.

You tackle uncertainty and risk by working hard to collect every bit of information possible. From tracking past performance to number crunching and creating what-if scenarios, you determine the least risky solution to your business challenge. Your investment in acquiring information helps you make smarter choices so you can be ultra-confident about the outcome. Once you are certain of your choice, you are willing to put everything on the line for it. To an outside observer, this behavior may seem risky, but to you, the decision is well-thought-through and thus carries no risk.

Risk-Takers are avid problem solvers. Your love for what you do and an intense desire to succeed keep you motivated to spend long hours working on a challenging problem. You solve problems analytically. Consequently, you can see patterns and make connections between seemingly unconnected phenomena. This gives you the ability to recognize opportunities and take advantage of market gaps before your competitors do.

As a Risk-Taker, you have a belief, sometimes exaggerated, in your ability to control the destiny and future of your venture. This internal locus of control motivates you to take action when things are not going well. You are quick to pursue alternative options when you encounter setbacks. Your will to win remains undiminished even after a painful defeat.

A word of caution: Some extremely successful Risk-Takers hold themselves in high regard. This phenomenon is known as *hyper-core self-evaluation* (hyper-CSE). An extreme positive self-assessment can lead these entrepreneurs to overestimate their ability to manage risk, underestimate the capital required to launch new (read: risky) initiatives, and underestimate the uncertainties or potential perils in the external business environment.

If you are a hyper-confident entrepreneur, you are certain that you can do no wrong and that you can resolve all problems if a decision turns bad. You are likely to engage in impulsive or uninformed risk taking, are less accurate in your forecast of success, and are more likely to persist in pursuing strategies even when they are not delivering the results you hoped for. In addition, hyper-CSE may lead to "shiny new object syndrome" — when you invest in multiple projects, overestimating your ability to get positive results from all of them, and in the process, end up hurting your core business.

Make sure to evaluate an opportunity rationally and thoroughly before taking action. Get feedback from people in your circle of trust. Take your time deciding which projects build on your core business and which are likely to take you off course. Keep the former, and get rid of the latter.

Risk-Taker in Action:

Bill Gates on Warren Buffett: "Warren doesn't outperform other investors because he computes odds better. That's not it at all. Warren never makes an investment where the difference between doing it and not doing it relies on the second digit of computation. He doesn't invest — take a swing of the bat — unless the opportunity appears unbelievably good."

Jeff Bezos, founder and CEO of Amazon.com: "Ninety-plus percent of the innovation at Amazon is incremental and critical and much less risky. We know how to open new product categories. We know how to open new geographies. That doesn't mean that these things are guaranteed to work, but we have a lot of expertise and a lot of knowledge. All of these things based on our operating history are things that we can analyze quantitatively rather than to have to make intuitive judgments."

Andy Dunn, co-founder and CEO of Bonobos: "Prior to a lobotomy I just underwent which removed shiny new object syndrome (SNOS) from my brain, I was both an asset and a threat to my own company. The company is trying to do one thing, and I would come up with another. I can't tell you how dangerous this is. If the founder doesn't know what the company is doing, the company won't either."

Maximizing Your Risk-Taker Talent:

1. *Know what you do know and what you do not know.* Understand the limits of your knowledge. Recognize the preferences and biases inherent in your worldview that can affect your judgment about the results you

expect. Resist predicting outcomes based on limited evidence. Gather all relevant information before you take action.

2. *Take risks incrementally.* When exploring a new venture, a new market, or a new product, minimize risks by making a small initial investment and evaluating the idea at successive stages in the development process. Consider it an experiment. Build a prototype, test the market, and collect information. Then decide if the idea is worth investing in further or abandoning.

3. *Beware of confirmation bias.* Your extremely positive self-image may lead you to favor information that confirms your beliefs and opinions, while discounting information that contradicts your viewpoint. Do not let this bias influence your decision making. Ask people with opposing views to counter your initial idea or concept. Considering different points of view as well as your own will help

you perceive opportunities more realistically and pick the ones with a higher probability of success.

4. *Construct different scenarios to guide your decision-making process.* Envision how things will unfold in the future, analyze the different directions a project can take, and estimate the outcomes in all directions. When you bring potential risk factors to light, you can choose the least risky path.

5. *Don't gamble.* Take careful calculated risks. Before an exciting idea sweeps you away in anticipation of what you will accomplish, impose a cooling-off period of a few weeks before you commit any funds. This will give you time to calculate the odds of success and put a plan in place to mitigate the risks.

6. *Kill unimportant projects.* You might overestimate your ability to succeed at multiple projects simultaneously. With your team, analyze all the projects in your company. Keep your focus on projects that strengthen and build on your core business. Ditch the rest.

REFERENCES

Please note that any statistics not cited stem from Gallup research and/or studies.

Part 1: Only Entrepreneurs Can Save America and the World By Jim Clifton

Abouzeid, R. (2011, January 21). *Bouazizi: The man who set himself and Tunisia on fire.* Time. Retrieved January 29, 2014, from http://www.time.com/time/world/article/0,8599,2043557,00.html

Acs, Z. (2006, Winter). How is entrepreneurship good for economic growth? *Innovations, 1*(1), 97-107.

Allan, N. (2013, October 23). *The real drivers of growth aren't small businesses—they're new businesses.* Retrieved February 13, 2014, from http://www.theatlantic.com/magazine/archive/2013/11/small-business-tall-tales/309533/

Brown, A. (2013, June 28). *Americans say economy is top worry for nation's future.* Retrieved January 17, 2014, from http://www.gallup.com/poll/163298/americans-say-economy-top-worry-nation-future.aspx

Desilver, D. (2013, June 7). *World's Muslim population more widespread than you might think*. Retrieved March 26, 2014, from http://www.pewresearch.org/fact-tank/2013/06/07/worlds-muslim-population-more-widespread-than-you-might-think/

Duttagupta, R., & Helbling, T. (2013, October 8). *Global growth patterns shifting, says IMF WEO*. Retrieved February 22, 2014, from https://www.imf.org/external/pubs/ft/survey/so/2013/new100813a.htm

Esposito, J.L., & Mogahed, D. (2007). *Who speaks for Islam? What a billion Muslims really think*. New York: Gallup Press.

Fisher, M. (2011, March 26). In Tunisia, act of one fruit vendor unleashes wave of revolution through Arab world. Retrieved January 25, 2014, from http://www.washingtonpost.com/world/in-tunisia-act-of-one-fruit-vendor-sparks-wave-of-revolution-through-arab-world/2011/03/16/AFjfsueB_story.html

Gallup & Operation HOPE. (2013). The 2013 Gallup-Hope Index. Retrieved February 4, 2014, from http://www.operationhope.org/images/uploads/Files/2013galluphopereport.pdf

Katz, B., & Wagner, J. (2014, February 17). *Innovation districts appear in cities as disparate as Montreal and London*. Retrieved February 28, 2014, from http://www.theguardian.com/local-government-network/2014/feb/17/innovation-cities-montreal-london-silicon-valley

Mensa International. (n.d.). About Mensa International. Retrieved May 5, 2014, from http://www.mensa.org/about-us

Mullen, M.G. (2011, February). *Senate armed services committee defense posture hearing*. Retrieved January 29, 2014, from http://www.dod.mil/dodgc/olc/docs/testMullen06152011.pdf

RT. (2012, July 16). *IMF cuts global growth forecast for 2013*. Retrieved February 8, 2014, from http://rt.com/business/imf0-cuts-global-growth-forecast-for-2013-289/

Tencer, D. (2011, October 25). *Innovation Cities Index 2011: Toronto named among 10 most innovative cities in the world*. Retrieved February 25, 2014, from http://www.huffingtonpost.ca/2011/10/25/innovation-cities-index-toronto_n_1030679.html

United States Census Bureau. (n.d.). *Longitudinal Research Database*. Retrieved January 28, 2014, from http://www.census.gov/econ/overview/ma0800.html

United States Census Bureau. (n.d.). *Statistics about business size (including small business) from the U.S. Census Bureau*. Retrieved January 28, 2014, from https://www.census.gov/econ/smallbus.html

United States Census Bureau. (n.d.). *U.S. and world population clock*. Retrieved February 14, 2014, from https://www.census.gov/popclock/

Young, J.T. (2013, April 12). *The worst four years of GDP growth in history: Yes, we should be worried*. Retrieved January 22, 2014, from http://www.forbes.com/sites/realspin/2013/04/12/the-worst-four-years-of-gdp-growth-in-history-yes-we-should-be-worried/

Part 2: What City Leaders Should Do Now
By Jim Clifton

U.S. Small Business Administration Office of Advocacy. (2012, September). *Frequently asked questions about small business*. Retrieved February 19, 2014, from http://www.sba.gov/sites/default/files/FAQ_Sept_2012.pdf

Part 3: The 10 Talents of Successful Entrepreneurs
By Sangeeta Bharadwaj Badal, Ph.D.

Bajarin, T. (2013, Feb. 11). *Has Apple finished disrupting markets?* Retrieved November 1, 2013, from http://techland.time.com/2013/02/11/has-apple-finished-disrupting-markets/

References

Campbell, A. (2013, September 5). *6 rules of entrepreneurship from founders in the trenches.* Retrieved January 29, 2014, from http://www.innovationamerica.us/index.php/ innovation-daily/32355-rules-of-entrepreneurship-from-founders-in-the-trenches?utm_source=innovation daily---your-daily-newsletter-highlighting-global-innovation-news-and-trends&utm_medium=gazetty&utm_campaign=09-09-2013

Chell, E., Haworth, J.M., & Brearley, S. (1991). *The entrepreneurial personality: Concepts, cases, and categories.* Hampshire, United Kingdom: Cengage Learning EMA.

Christensen, C.M., & Raynor, M.E. (2003). *The innovator's solution: Creating and sustaining successful growth.* Boston: Harvard Business School Publishing.

Collins, C.J., Hanges, P.J., & Locke, E.A. (2004). The relationship of achievement motivation to entrepreneurial behavior: A meta-analysis. *Human Performance, 17*(1), 95-117.

Dell, M., & Fredman, C. (1999). *Direct from Dell: Strategies that revolutionized an industry.* New York: HarperBusiness.

Deutschman, A. (2004, August 1). *Inside the mind of Jeff Bezos.* Retrieved January 29, 2014, from http://www.fastcompany.com/50541/inside-mind-jeff-bezos

Dunn, A. (2013, May 27). *Start-up drugs.* Retrieved January 9, 2014, from https://medium.com/what-i-learned-building/922fdc3a57c8

Dyson, J. (2005, September). James Dyson on innovation. *Ingenia, 24,* 31-34.

Gladwell, M. (2009, July 27). *Cocksure: Banks, battles, and the psychology of overconfidence.* Retrieved November 6, 2013, from http://www.newyorker.com/reporting/2009/07/27/090727fa_fact_gladwell?currentPage=all

Guber, P. (2011). *Tell to win: Connect, persuade, and triumph with the hidden power of story.* New York: Crown Business.

Harley-Davidson Motor Company. (2012, September 10). *Harley-Davidson calls on fans to unleash their own personal freedom and independence.* Retrieved January 9, 2014, from http://investor.harley-davidson.com/mobile.view?c=87981&v=203&d=1&id=1733717

Hiller, N.J., & Hambrick, D.C. (2005). Conceptualizing executive hubris: the role of (hyper-)core self-evaluations in strategic decision-making. *Strategic Management Journal, 26*(4). 297-319.

Joel. (2013, March 10). *20 unstoppable entrepreneurs share their advice for success.* Retrieved January 7, 2014, from http://addicted2success.com/success-advice/20-unstoppable-entrepreneurs-share-their-advice-for-success/

Loewenstein, G. (1992). The fall and rise of psychological explanations in the economics of intertemporal choice. In G. Loewenstein & J. Elster (Eds.), *Choice over time.* New York: Russell Sage.

Loomis, C. (2012). *Tap dancing to work: Warren Buffett on practically everything, 1966-2012: A Fortune magazine book*. New York: Portfolio/Penguin.

Lowe, J. (2007). *Warren Buffett speaks: Wit and wisdom from the world's greatest investor*. Hoboken, NJ: Wiley.

Luchies, M. (2013, September 4). *Starting a business as a young entrepreneur: Interview with Sachin Kamdar, CEO of Parse.ly*. Retrieved March 26, 2014, from http://under30ceo.com/succeeding-over-obstacles-interview-with-sachin-kamdar-ceo-of-parse-ly/

Manjoo, F. (2011, August 1). *"People will misunderstand you."* Retrieved January 29, 2014, from http://www.slate.com/articles/technology/top_right/2011/08/people_will_misunderstand_you.html

Meyer, G.J., Finn, S.E., Eyde, L.D., Kay, G.G., Moreland, K.L., Dies, R.R., et al. (2001). Psychological testing and psychological assessment: A review of evidence and issues. *American Psychologist, 56*(2), 128-65.

Mitchell, J.R., & Shepherd, D.A. (2010, January). To thine own self be true: Images of self, images of opportunity, and entrepreneurial action. *Journal of Business Venturing, 25*(1), 138-154.

Nicolaou, N., & Shane, S. (2009). Can genetic factors influence the likelihood of engaging in entrepreneurial activity? *Journal of Business Venturing, 24*(1), 1-22.

Nicolaou, N., & Shane, S. (2010). Entrepreneurship and occupational choice: Genetic and environmental influences. *Journal of Economic Behavior & Organization, 76,* 3-14.

Ogilvy, D. (2012). *Confessions of an advertising man.* London: Southbank.

Oreskovic, A. (2012, April 5). *Google CEO touts gains, focuses on long term bets.* Retrieved May 9, 2014, from http://www.reuters.com/article/2012/04/05/net-us-google-idUSBRE83418220120405

Oxford, J. (2013, September 24). *6 things online retailers can learn from Amazon.* Retrieved January 29, 2014, from http://www.forbes.com/sites/groupthink/2013/09/24/6-things-online-retailers-can-learn-from-amazon/

Plous, S. (1993). *The psychology of judgment and decision making.* New York: McGraw-Hill.

Preston, J. (n.d.). *10 inspirational Richard Branson quotes.* Retrieved January 7, 2014, from http://www.virgin.com/entrepreneur/10-inspirational-richard-branson-quotes

Prive, T. (2013, May 5). *Top 32 quotes every entrepreneur should live by.* Retrieved January 7, 2014, from http://www.forbes.com/sites/tanyaprive/2013/05/02/top-32-quotes-every-entrepreneur-should-live-by/

References

Pulli, K., Karma, K., Norio, R., Sistonen, P., Goring, H.H.H., & Jarvela, I. (2008). Genome-wide linkage scan for loci of musical aptitude in Finnish families: Evidence for a major locus at 4q22. *Journal of Medical Genetics*, *45*(7), 451-456.

Rauch, A., & Frese, M. (2007). Let's put the person back into entrepreneurship research: A meta-analysis on the relationship between business owners' personality traits, business creation, and success. *European Journal of Work and Organizational Psychology*, *16*(4), 353-385.

Rauch, A., & Frese, M. (2012). Born to be an entrepreneur? Revisiting the personality approach to entrepreneurship. In: J.R. Baum, M. Frese, & R.A. Baron (Eds.), *The Psychology of Entrepreneurship*. New York: Psychology Press.

Salter, C. (2008, February 19). *Marissa Mayer's 9 principles of innovation*. Retrieved January 9, 2014, from http://www. fastcompany.com/702926/marissa-mayers-9-principles-innovation

Simpson, M. (2011, October 30). *A sister's eulogy for Steve Jobs*. Retrieved November 20, 2013, from http://www.nytimes. com/2011/10/30/opinion/mona-simpsons-eulogy-for-steve-jobs. html?pagewanted=1&_r=1

Sitkin, S.B. (1992). Learning through failure: the strategy of small losses. *Research in Organizational Behavior*, *14*, 231-266.

Stenner, T. (2012, May 30). *The secret to success? Intellectual curiosity.* Retrieved May 9, 2014, from http://www.theglobeandmail.com/globe-investor/investment-ideas/the-secret-to-success-intellectual-curiosity/article4217614/

Stewart, B. (2011, Fall). The human internet. *Utah Valley Business Q*, 18-25. Retrieved March 26, 2014, from http://utahvalleybusinessq.com/fall2011/18.html

Stewart, W.H., & Roth, P.L. (2004). Data quality affects meta-analytic conclusions: A response to Miner and Raju (2004) concerning entrepreneurial risk propensity. *Journal of Applied Psychology, 89*(1), 14-21.

Stoltz, P.G. (1999). *Adversity quotient: Turning obstacles into opportunities.* Hoboken, NJ: Wiley.

Strauss, K. (2013, May 5). *Billionaire Ronald Perelman spends $100M to teach entrepreneurs.* Retrieved February 2, 2014, from http://www.forbes.com/sites/karstenstrauss/2013/05/03/billionaire-ronald-perelman-spends-100m-to-teach-entrepreneurs/

Taylor, B. (2012, April 4). *It's not what you sell, it's what you believe.* Retrieved November 1, 2013, from http://blogs.hbr.org/2012/04/its-not-what-you-sell-its-what/

ACKNOWLEDGEMENTS

We would like to thank everyone who made this book possible. It began with Don Clifton's pioneering theory of strengths and his focus on improving lives with greater emphasis on what's *right* with people, rather than on what's wrong with them. His work of more than five decades, which included his focus on the psychology of the entrepreneur, became the foundation for the Entrepreneurial StrengthsFinder (ESF) assessment and this book. Our deepest gratitude to Don for teaching us to soar with our strengths.

Many have generously given their time and talent to develop the entrepreneurship initiative at Gallup. We would like to recognize Geoff Brewer, editor extraordinaire, who deftly merged two author voices into a coherent narrative. Jennifer Robison, for her brilliance with words and a genius for editing and rewriting. Seth Schuchman, Tim Dean, and the entire team at Gallup Press for navigating the deep and sometimes choppy waters of publishing with ease and élan and maintaining the highest levels of quality throughout the production process. Further, we are grateful to Kelly Henry for her masterful editing and collaboration on multiple text rewrites. Thanks to Trista Kunce and Jessica Stutzman for their patient and thorough fact checking of several drafts of this book. Thanks to Beth Karadeema for her aesthetic book design — and along with Chin-Yee Lai — another striking Gallup Press book cover.

This work would not have been possible without the cumulative brilliance and knowledge of our exceptionally talented psychologists and scientists. First and foremost, thanks to Joe Streur, with whom we have had the extraordinary good fortune to collaborate and learn from while developing the ESF. Our long discussions about entrepreneurial intent and process and shared thinking about the causes of successful entrepreneurship have extended our understanding of this research. We would also like to thank Jim Harter, Yongwei Yang, and Jim Asplund, who influenced our thinking and guided us through the difficult and sometimes frustrating path of quantitative analysis.

Our sincere thanks to Phil Ruhlman and Jim Krieger for their invaluable wisdom, big-picture thinking, and unwavering belief in this project. Huge kudos to Todd Johnson and Joe Daly for their tireless commitment to the ESF project and for setting the direction of Gallup's Entrepreneurship and Job Creation practice. Scott Wright and Bryant Ott spent endless hours, days, and weeks crafting perfect content for the ESF report and website. Jamie Konwinski and her team designed the online platform for the ESF project. And thanks to Adrienne Ott for keeping all of us in line and on task, moving from one milestone to the next in perfect harmony. Thanks also to Gerardo Aranda and the Mexico team.

Many thanks to great business builders Roy Spence and Paul Allen, who generously shared their experiences as successful entrepreneurs with us. Their quotes and insights dot the book — as do the learnings from thousands of entrepreneurs across the U.S. who completed the ESF assessment and allowed us to research and study their talents.

Finally, we would like thank our families for their endless patience and support through long months of book writing. And thanks to our colleagues and friends at Gallup for inspiring us to continue the strengths journey.

ABOUT THE AUTHORS

Jim Clifton is Chairman and CEO of Gallup and author of *The Coming Jobs War*. His most recent innovation, the Gallup World Poll, is designed to give the world's 7 billion citizens a voice in virtually all key global issues. Under Clifton's leadership, Gallup has expanded from a predominantly U.S.-based company to a worldwide organization with 40 offices in 30 countries and regions.

Sangeeta Bharadwaj Badal, Ph.D., is the primary researcher for Gallup's Entrepreneurship and Job Creation initiative. Dr. Badal is responsible for translating research findings into interventions that drive small-business growth. She is the author of the book *Gender, Social Structure and Empowerment: Status Report of Women in India*. Dr. Badal earned her doctorate in anthropology and geography from the University of Nebraska-Lincoln (UNL).

Gallup Press exists to educate and inform the people who govern, manage, teach, and lead the world's 7 billion citizens. Each book meets Gallup's requirements of integrity, trust, and independence and is based on Gallup-approved science and research.

GALLUP E-BOOKS APP

Get your favorite Gallup books — now on your mobile devices.

- Read popular Gallup Press e-book titles right on your phone or tablet

- Free download

- Available for iPhone, iPad, and Android

Download the free Gallup E-Books app now!

GALLUP® E-Books